Executive Protection
A buyer's guide

Dr. James Willer

Copyright © 2012 James Willer PhD

All rights reserved.

ISBN:1542635802
ISBN-13:9781542635806

DEDICATION
Precision Dynamics Group

I walk a path filled with rocks

My moccasins are worn and torn

Feet hurt like hell but still I walk the path

Angels call me by name but still I walk

My buddies and my gun give me some comfort

For there is no greater good than to lay down your life in defense of others

I've followed the moral code

Defend those who cannot defend themselves

Then I die

Belief and faith say there is more

I will sit on the left side of God

My buddies and my gun I still walk the path

We will protect heaven from the evils of the world

With my gun and my buddies

TABLE OF CONTENTS

Introduction

The purpose of this book is not an attempt to save you money, instead it is meant to educate you on the executive protection field. When spending money for executive protection, my goal is to help you to get your money's worth. It is like the analogy of buying a diamond ring; you may not get a quality diamond if you base your decision making on picking the largest shiny rock available. Instead you need the latest available diamond education before you go out shopping.

My style of writing for this book will be in the form of general conversation. I am the author of this book but by no means a highly experienced professional writer. I realized a long time ago that I could not be perfect at everything that I attempted to do in life but it has never stopped me from trying new things. Some of my greatest life learning events have occurred when I failed to be perfect. This book may not be a perfect literary work worthy of the best seller list, but I guarantee it will contain valuable information for you.

What is executive protection?

Executive protection as defined for this writing as providing personal security at a higher level than the minimal security standard. An executive protection team operates similar to that of elite Special Forces personnel do for the military. It is the best of the best, dedicated to protecting the lives of others even at their own risk. The special individuals tasked for this job form a team that trains to exceed basic high standards. They function in the realm of uncharted physical and mental levels. Most executive protection teams operate on short duration missions when a threat of violence is highly probable. They are not meant for the daily security guard, long term standing at a post, type of work.

Modern threats require modern solutions. The internet and social media have added new dimensions to the security realm. The news media covers violent acts overseas in great detail, giving innovative ideas to potential threats. In the past, we focused on the handgun as the main weapon of choice that bad guys would be using. Now we worry about automatic rifles and car bombs just like the military has had to deal with. The new problem being confronted by security teams is providing a higher level of security within the current American socially acceptable environment instead of a combat zone.

Just another training day

As always, I got to the shooting range early, had a little truck stop coffee and I was good to go. After the morning shooting drills we started movement drills and a box formation. There was a good-looking woman picked for the acting principle, the one for us to get our hands on professionally. We were protecting the principle in the middle of our formation. We started moving, a flash bang went off, and the dance begins. There is confusion on direction not seeing the loud bang. Still you work as a team going off the reactions and commands of other members. On purpose this drill is meant to be confusing. The training officer is screaming to move, move, and keep moving. Another flash bang goes off, this time very close. Training has us moving the principle into a vehicle to get them out of the area. Protecting the person in the middle is of the most important objective. The protective team has people dictated by the type of threat to react without thought or delay. Part of the unit is assigned to engage the threat.

As spring loaded metal targets rise up representing the threat, gun fire starts. I cannot even explain the number of shots unleashed in seconds on multiple targets. All rounds without exception must hit the target. I heard a voice over the noise hollering, "Get that damn finger off the trigger guard or I will cut it off". I screamed, "roger that". Into the vehicle we were moving the principle and driving out of the threat area is the next action to perform. One person is down representing a medical emergency under a threat. Commands are given to cover the wounded, and reload. All this is going on under the training officer yelling at us. I dropped my empty magazine on the chest of the wounded team member, looking down I smile and say, "I got you covered but I am not going to ruin those fine pants you wear by dragging your fat ass out of here.

The shooting is over and principle being protected is long gone. I heard, "Ok, who shot the hostage target in the arm?" "Wasn't me", I said. "See that little group in between the bad guy's eyes, those are mine". "Yes, but that one in the heart, is

that yours? The bad guy had the hostage's arm over his heart.
The hostage just got shot in the arm, let's try it again. This
time let's get it right people, he said." Six hours more of
training to go and loving it. I am part of a team, where one
member has an entire wall full of shooting awards, one with a
PhD, and another with a master's degree in computer fraud.
Other members forming this team had been police officers, a
black belt, or should I say they are basically just a fine group
of bad asses who know how to run a gun.

A good Team Dynamic

So what blend of people make up a good team dynamic? For a
team to effectively move a principal in and out of the building
or vehicle, a lot of groundwork has to be done first. You have
to plan for everything evil and bad that can possibly happen.
If you can think of it, then it can happen. The more experience
you have the more what-ifs you can generate along with
hopefully more effective solutions. Dealing with the
unexpected is what you're trying to avoid. No matter how well
you do this planning, there can be events no one saw coming.
Team members must embrace change without missing a beat.
Adaptability under stress is a fundamental quality all team
members must have.

The team unit trains to react to a threat, cut fractions of a
second off of reaction times, to shoot fast yet shrink the shot
group size. The object is to excel way beyond good enough,
trying to constantly improve. Knowing that under stress, our
reaction times change, we train with the thought that whatever
our shooting times end up like, we can still improve.

You can only have one team leader in an effective team. If the team has internal conflicts, when under stress, that dynamic will be magnified. Even worse, the principal may be affected negatively. The principle should only have to deal with the communication from one leader in charge at any given time. The leader should present as a friendly reassuring person very much in control. This person will be giving the team firm confident directions and provide timely direct communication to the principal. The rest of the team should be focused and serious not directing individual personal communication to the principal. The officer in charge should be detail oriented and focused attention to the moment.

This team leader may have a lot of questions for the principle which appear unrelated to the project but during the start up phase, it is very important to the event planning. This team should have contacts with police departments, different law-enforcement agencies, area hospitals, and they should have local contacts. These important local contacts are like restaurant owners or businesses that maybe accessed. There should be alternative route planning with all of these things readily available and preset before anything is moved. This work load is sometimes avoided by some companies but is vitally important to a quality team assignment with all members doing their part.

What qualities are you looking for?

As long as you are not a celebrity, the general principles you're looking for when picking an executive protection team are qualified professional appeal and the ability to operate unnoticed. You will also look at operational history and the level of training the team maintains. It is important that this group of protectors has a track record of working for large companies rather than just individuals. There is not a true representation of skill level just by dropping names of celebrities. Those teams that have worked for high level companies have a much stronger vetting process. If a high dollar company has picked this group for executive protection, you can bet that they have been vetted thoroughly. A unit that is thoroughly versed in executive protection probably has worked with healthcare companies as well. This type of protection need is a totally different work experience than needed for Hollywood. Healthcare can encompass extreme emotional trauma, and must be dealt with differently than other clients.

 Just to clarify some terms I am using, the difference between client and principle is the client is the buyer or the person purchasing the security. The principle is the one being protected.   This can easily be two different people.

During the pre-interview process, expect questions about your health, allergies, medications, and any medical conditions that might limit balance and movement. These sorts of questions are very important for the principle's safety. The entire team is responsible for the safety of the principal at all times even if this is personal medical reasons. This can include natural causes such as a heart condition, drug use, or equilibrium problems. During the pre-interview process you have to be open and truthful about things you may not want to talk about such as drug and alcohol problems, things you normally would not relate to others. For the team responsibility, they become very important to the preparation process. As an example, small details such as where you keep your allergy medication can make a large impact on the speed that the medication can be applied during an emergency.

Presentation of the Ideal Resume'

Sometimes the presentation of the skill set of a protection team does not match up with the type of protection needed. It can also not reflect reality. Most people working in executive protection have a Resume' that can appear very impressive. It is important that you look a little deeper into the true background of these resumes. Who are they in reality; separate from the bravado and verbiage. What is being put out sometimes does not match up with the true skill and experience levels. In the military we had different jobs, (MOS) method of service, that can range everywhere from laundry service to water purification or even Special Operations. Within Special Operations there are administrative positions and non-combat roles. Either way, a person can state they were a gun carrier for protection reasons while serving in the military. What you actually did can vary greatly in skill building experience when it comes to things like conflict resolution. Experience dealing with an indigenous population for example or being shot at can be skill builders. In different types of violent environments that the military might put a person into, these events can shape a personality. How you reacted to these conditions can vary greatly depending on your personality. These reactions can range from curling up into a ball in the corner to uncontrolled fighting wild.

On my last appointment with the military I met four people whose resume will show they worked border security for the army alongside the military police. Two of them have been driving trucks in Afghanistan and the other two were cooks based in the United States. The two army truck drivers were skilled professionals. I would have no problem training them up for what I do. The other two are a different story all together. These two were the most bizarre incompetent posers I have ever come across in the military. After one year all four had military border security listed on the resume. Their resume is not going to tell you which two you want to hire.

Every male that has a respectable level of testosterone, every male who has ever played football, wrestled, boxed, or actually any sport that is competitive, sees themselves as being able to do executive protection. Any martial artist who has achieve the level of black belt in any style even the pretty dancing style ones, feel they can expertly do executive protection. Anyone who has been in the military, not dependent on the branch of service; as long as they were in the military feel they are more than qualified to market themselves for executive protection.

Some see themselves as macho enough to do executive protection if they worked security, law-enforcement, or as dispatcher for a police department. Almost anybody within this particular community sees themselves as able to do executive protection. Anyone who has worked in a bar or has had to deal with conflict within that bar sees themselves as able to do executive protection. Anyone who can shoot a firearm respectively sees themselves as being able to do executive protection. Any former or current cowboy, farmer, survivalist, even any exceptional physically fit person can see themselves as more than qualified to provide executive protection. If you don't believe me, just ask them.

Let me state that this is a generalization, not a statement to cover 100% of any given population. Think about the percentage of macho individuals, larger than normal males, who do not even fit in the above categories that see themselves as being able to do executive protection. Please do not let me forget the group that has been tapped several times for high profile music events. It is those who wear a black leather jacket and ride a Harley Davidson motorcycle as members of an outlaw gang. So what have we learned from the above information so far? We learned that military, law-enforcement, public notoriety, and security background is good for a basis to start from, but only from a background starting point.

Large security companies; not what you think

Within security jobs and security personal, there is an extensive range of educational backgrounds and needed skills. A security guard could come in to this type of business with a GED and have never been in a fight in their life. Another guard could come in as a retired police officer that had worked the inner-city for years holding a masters degree in criminal justice. Both can be working a security post side-by-side on any given day. With these two individuals you could not tell skill levels just by saying they are working security. What type of individual you're getting requires a more complex investigation. The same variation holds true within civilian law-enforcement. There is a vast difference in skill levels within law-enforcement as well. Police are a significant step up from base line security but there is a big difference between their individual skills, strength, and fighting ability.

As an example of the variety of security guards on a post, I will give you the following three security guards: a woman 5 foot two and 240 pounds, a male martial arts expert, or a senior citizen handicapped retired cook. All the above examples can represent the same status and rank within any particular security post. The same can hold true for the local police. Both have the same pedigree within the law enforcement community but when it comes to a direct drop down drag it out fight, a specific type officer can be at a disadvantage by size or experience. Individuals exist within the military, martial arts, security, and law-enforcement communities that have never been tested under fire. There can be a big gap in experience and age as well. Some individuals have high strung personalities while others are very calm professionals.

Out of all these security type people some know exactly how they will react under stress or under fire. Others have no idea how they will react if they were ever threatened by an angry individual or even shot at. Working a protection detail for you is not the time to find out. If you watch how the federal government Secret Service works, they place the new personal in the background with the experienced agents up front. Over time, the experience will develop the young agents move into a more reliable asset position.

To further provide you with a little depth on this subject, security officers come in many flavors and styles. A security company will hire new officers based on their ability to observe and report. That would be their ability to see something and to vocalize what they have seen. In most cases, no more than that is wanted and any more may be illegal for the officer to participate in. Uniforms and guns are for image only just to generalize on the subject. They are meant to project the feeling of security for a client and principle. Ever wonder why an officer patrolling a shopping mall in a security vehicle has their lights flashing? It is so the shoppers sees them and feels secure. Believe me, the professional bad guy loves knowing where security is. Basically the security company is hiring people to stand around watching everybody like a mobile security camera. These guards project a professional image that no camera can do. It gives the public a feeling that they are being protected.

Let me give you an example of this security imagery when you hire a large security company to provide executive protection for you. They will pick security guards from their pool of people that are legally qualified to protect you and also project the correct image. I have never seen a person being picked for this duty due to their skill level. If this was you as the client or principle, what caliber person did you just get? I have personally seen a large security company post a licensed private investigator to guard a executive toilet and pick another person with no investigative experience or training to do a investigator position. This decision was based on friendship, status, and image only. How do you know if you are getting from the large security companies a security guard who had to go to the range three different times to meet the minimum standard, or maybe the newly released police officer who could not meet police standards? I would prefer that you get a skill level that meets your needs.

Security officers get paid about a dollar an hour above minimum wage, but that is not what customers will be paying the large security company for their use. Their administrative fees can more than raise the cost to the client four times. Also, the price does not mean it guarantees an outstanding security professional. Working on a post day after day for years, the officer maybe highly motivated to accept any change to their job when it is offered. The true highly qualified skilled officers are few and far between. Those type officers have a tendency to move on to higher paying jobs after a short period of time. The ones left are the ones being grabbed for the executive protection assignment from existing posts. Another point I could make here is that there might be a tendency to pick the officer that if removed from their post creates the least amount of problem for day to day staffing. In other words, they are picking the one with the lowest value to the current job. Some large security companies already know this can cause a staffing problem. So to fix this, they might take a cut of the money being offered, and sub-contract the work out to groups such as Precision Dynamics Group, one who specialize in executive protection. Some of these companies realize that it only takes one incident going wrong to ruin a reputation. Individuals not trained to the level needed for the job is a disaster waiting to happen.

When a company hires a large number of individuals, they must verify the truth of the new hires background. The risk of hiring a terrorist for a sensitive post is a possibility. As an example of the quality to these checks some of the large security companies' deal with, I will give you a resent personal experience. I was employed at one of the largest security companies in the world and had been working for them for around five months. I received a phone call from the company needing some additional information from me. This was from their main corporate office. In conversation, they informed me that during the time period I had been employed with them one of my references had expired, in other words had died. I was very aware of this having attended the funeral. They had talked to his wife who gave me a glowing reference but it wasn't the original individual I had listed for them. They also had a couple other issues or bones to pick with me. One was with my required military documents. They were confused with the timetable of military years served. It was because of this fact that there were dates listed at same time with a civilian job. The person doing the checks and references did not understand what the National Guard was or how it functioned. He also did not understand how the structure of State and Federal government worked. He was hired from overseas and was the only one doing the background checks. I went through three different phone conversations until I reach a high enough supervisor that understood government and military structure. The lady immediately said," Oh never mind, thank you very much for your service, we need nothing from you." I tell this story to illustrate the level of assurance you are getting a fully vetted and screened individual from some of the large security companies. It appeared I had been working at a sensitive armed post for five months before they got around to calling my references. It wasn't long after that this same large company got a small subset of the company to go through the local ranks looking for anybody that was qualified to carry a gun and had my name on the list. Their main criteria were that I had been in the military, licensed to carry a gun, and had the right look, nothing more than that. The company wanted to staff an executive protection position for a local job.

To follow up on this line on how quality individuals are picked for different positions, there was a large civil protest in one of the major southern cities within the United States. A large global security company had people staffed in the area that had come to the area to observe the protest. They wanted to learn whatever they could from the event and I do not fault them for that in any way. They brought in their high level corporate personnel from out-of-state and from overseas to observe the protest. This group was focused on how security personnel reacted and dealt with this version of civil unrest. I had the privilege to stand beside the corporate elements and listening to their conversation. During this time period, one of the executives noticed there were three individuals providing security between the protesters and a well known national news organization. He said, "We need to do that, we can pay a couple of dollars more to our armed personnel and market them for those positions." It wasn't long after that a call went out to the local ranks looking for armed personnel. They needed volunteers for a short-term contract doing executive protection for the company. These were the same personnel that were not qualified to carry handcuffs, OC spray, or batons, standard police equipment. They had no additional training, no hands-on training, nothing extra other than the image of standing in front of an executive toilet in a bank. The company ended up having staffing issues with these chosen personnel. As an example of the problems, the security personnel would not show up to work as scheduled. Within short order, they decided to go with a higher quality of individual. The company then focused on personnel that had basic law-enforcement training. The only problem with this idea was that there was not enough of that type of trained individual available. Most were already employed at a higher pay level. The executive protection jobs were then sub-contracted out to groups that specialize in executive protection. Of course, they kept a percentage of the contracted money as a job finder's fee.

Good police officers are hard to find

Basic law enforcement training produces individuals who are licensed and qualified to be a police officer. If they can get hired by a local police agency, it will be at a much higher level of pay than offered by security companies. Individuals who cannot get hired as a police officer, security companies will hire them at a higher pay than a basic security guard. It will be well under police officer pay though. As a general statement, police trained individuals working for security companies are for some reason unable to meet the minimum standard to get jobs with police agencies.

An active-duty law enforcement officer can provide you with a much higher level of protection but I have met police officers from big cities who could not fight or shoot their way out of a paper bag. They are officers because they have met the minimum standard for skills and diversity required by law to become a police officer. In one state, the shooting standard for police was lower than for an armed security guard. What I'm getting at is just because you work for a dance troupe doesn't mean you're a professional dancer. Just because you wear the badge and have a gun doesn't mean that you have a skill level above the minimum requirement.

Bouncers with skills, but do they meet the job requirements

There is an art form to defusing a violent or life threatening situation. To be able to confront a conflict with control requires a soft approach to start with. There can be the application of a basic smile and then there is a comforting smile. There is a smile that can elicit conflict or one to calm a situation. How you project can either make somebody become more aggressive or less aggressive. You can stick your chest out as a challenge, assured you are ending up in a fight or use body position to represent authority. Do you really want to escalate to a violent outcome or defuse and defect allowing for an escape for both parties.

When you are protecting somebody, you need to be able to move the principle out of the area immediately. What you are confronting as a threat, whatever the problem, is a type of de-escalation or defusing. It is definitely an art form. Commonly a bar bouncer, somebody who works at eliminating threats in a drinking establishment, do this on a daily basis.

 I worked as a bouncer when I was in college. It was a bar called Big Al's in Wayne Nebraska. I worked with a very large individual, six-foot four inches of 400 pounds, known as Big Rick. He was great to work with, easy-going; we worked together great as a team. I would hit them, pushing them into Rick, and he would then crush them. Great teamwork is hard to find as Rick and I found many ways not to fight in the first place.

Violence is not what is wanted by the establishment where

you're working. To de-escalate from a physical fight occurring or to prevent conflict from growing, is what you trying to do. Violent conflict within the establishment creates a bad image that can lower revenues. This will keep people from wanting to come to that establishment where they may find troublemakers or be threatened. Within bar crowds, this type of environment draws many different type individuals. You are going to find locals, outsiders, and troublemakers. You're going to also have drunks to deal with. Each different group has to be handled differently in order to defuse whatever is going on. Behavior patterns of the different groups require a different technique to deal with the problem. When using martial arts techniques in this environment, it is advisable not to hit, kick, or go to the ground. Manipulation of movement is the best choice in most cases. Remember that image is all important for de-escalation. Wrestling around on the ground it's not the type of fighting you want to do in a bar. Manipulation without violence is a start on being able to escort the individual to the exit. Moving them out of the conflict area without people noticing and without violence is always the best solution. It is a low level of control to start with and as you need more control, you upgrade towards more violent responses. The desire of the bar management is to have their bouncers fight without fighting.

Here are two examples of different situations that occurred to me as a bouncer. I had a drunk one Saturday night threatening me with a pool stick and it became a potentially very dangerous situation. I tried to talk to the person but because of his inebriation state, mitigating conversation wasn't going to go anywhere. I could not get close enough to grab the individual because he was armed basically with a club type weapon. I chose to take a pool ball and gently applied it to the back of his hand that he had placed on the pool table. Okay maybe not so gentle of an application but he decided to exit as I had requesting him to do. Another time at the end of the Saturday night normal partying, there was a drunk in a booth that the owner wanted me to remove out to the street. I applied a basic martial art hand hold even though he was drunk. There is still enough pain response that he was able to get to his feet and walk on his own to the front door. That technique looked totally nonviolent as opposed to the other technique earlier with the pool ball. I was able to avoid the potential extreme violence at the pool table, but a big difference exists between the public images that are projected between the two examples.

Getting a kick out of Martial Arts

Next, let us look at the reality versus projected image of a Taekwondo instructor as our martial art example. Taekwondo is a martial art that teaches kicking primarily. The high kicks which are this art forms specialty, are not really street applicable. A fifth degree black belt in Taekwondo can be easily dispatched out in a real life fight because the techniques that work out in the street are not taught in the Taekwondo school. When studying a formal martial art such as Taekwondo you are given rules to follow. You are not supposed to kick anybody between the legs, poke him in the eyes, or hit him in the throat. You take the school rules and go to tournaments for your real fight practice. For years you fight tournaments and you feel that you can kick your way to glory. When you fight out in the street, there are no rules and the best techniques to use are the ones not allowed in the tournament. That is why there is a big gap between the ability to fight out on the street and a formal martial art tournament fight. Executive protection is not the time to find out if you can handle yourself in a real street fight.

I was fighting a tournament in Fort Wayne Indiana back in the1980s. It was a karate organization that allowed kicks below the belt, something not seen in most martial arts. Let's just say this was when the karate fighter getting a point for a between the legs shot. I started the fight setting up against my opponent by doing a little shimmy shake dance and shoulder dip when I noticed my opponent moved his left foot outward. Along with the foot movement the leg moved outward opening the groin. When I did that right-hand fake shimmy I was thinking I was going to end this fight very quickly. We were circling when I faked a right hand with the left shoulder dip. He reacted as predicted and I proceeded to punt him like a football though the goal posts. His feet came up off the canvas but he came back down smiling at me. I seriously freaked out and almost lost the fight over it. He took my best kick to a very sensitive area and was still standing upright smiling.

Later sitting in a Pizza Hut restaurant, I discussed the subject with my coach and the other professional fighters there. They said there is no cortex in the brain to except the signal pleasure and pain, thus both were emotions and emotions can be crossed up. Have you heard of sadomasochism? It is where you get pleasure from pain. Give them a little pain followed by a little pleasure and the brain uses the signal pain for anticipation of the coming pleasure. It crosses up the normal emotion response. I had given him great pleasure but he will have difficulty sitting down the next day. Physical damage is still physical damage when it comes to application of force.

You do not want this crossing up of emotional processing found in martial arts used within executive protection. The looking forward to a fight or pain can cause even a subconscious behavioral change to set in. This can create a conflict with people where there was no need for it. It is like people who get pleasurable feedback off of creating drama. They have a slightly different behavior pattern because they want the start of conflict for entertainment purposes. Others may exhibit some type of hero/ victim syndrome or an "I want to be seen as special" need. Also conflict can be created to enhance a respect position when it would have never happened otherwise. This can come in the form of ego status or just getting noticed. This type of person is seeking pleasure from the negative which is never good thing in executive protection.

Old school shooting standards

My first executive protection job was with the U.S. Army around 1975 at Fort Polk Louisiana. I was assigned to cover the Secretary of State, Howard Calloway and the Secretary of the Army; I think his name is General Rogers. There were

some lesser known four-star generals in assemble but I paid
little attention to them. They pick me not because of my
ruggedly good looks, charm, and god-given massive size, but
because my assigned partner and I were the best shots in the
military police company. Along with this protection detail we
had to attend a formal banquet, direct some traffic, and
functioned as a tour guide for the more important people. Not
a bad day for a young Iowa boy new to the military. I would
have never been in that role had it not been generated from my
skill set developed growing up.

A few years before the above event, on just an average sunny
Saturday afternoon in small-town Midwest America the phone
rang. The local businessman said to have James grab the M-1
carbine because a bull or male cow got loose from the
meatpacking plant and is heading his way. I was 14 years old
at the time and weighed 130 pounds wet, a fine specimen of
asthmatic refinement. There I stood with an old 30 cal. M1
carbine rifle that had a reputation for being too small to shoot
people with during the Korean War. I was going to be faced
off with 2000 pounds of slightly angry bull and he did have
that angry look on his face. He was standing on second base in
the middle of the town's baseball field as if waiting for the
game to start. Gene yelled shoot him between the eyes, so

that's exactly what I did. Straight to the ground that beast fell. The importance of bullet placement was etched on my brain from that time on. I also learn that to miss may have resulted in my death. No amount of anabolic steroids and weightlifting could have saved that bovine from that well-placed shot, or me from placing that shot correctly. It was a very important life lesson I learned.

I grew up in Brunsville, a small town in Iowa, not far from the South Dakota border. The shooting standards in the region are a little different out on the prairie. My mother taught me how to shoot a gun and my father gave us limited ammunition, two bullets at a time, to teach us hunting skills. We were assigned to go out and bring back supper with only two chances. The objective was to learn hunting skills good enough to get close to your future meal. This method was intended so you would not miss. If done correctly, this leaves one shot to go play with. When you're limited on ammunition it's a totally different standard to meet than military shooting and the, it is close enough, standard. My brothers and my neighbors were all very competitive as we learned about life. It was a competition in which you could never shoot good enough. An example of the standards that we set over time were you had to be able to take a 22 rifle and hit 1/2 gallon milk carton at one hundred yards or a one gallon container with a 45 pistol at 200 yards. I know this doesn't mean anything to a non shooter but I included the numbers for the shooters reading the book. We shot open sites with an original 1886 Winchester at 800 yards, hitting at 2 foot circle. My brother recently used a modern civilian version of an M-16 rifle to shoot a four shot grouping the size of three inches at 300 yards. He did this with open sights, not even using a scoped rifle. Let me just say it is a high standard to meet. In the military the standard is a soldier trying to use that same type of rifle to hit a three foot circle at the same distance. It is two totally different accomplishments and a perfect example of meeting the minimum required level of skill to pass the objective. There was never a minimalist attitude in small town Iowa. You could never over perfect yourself or stop continuing to strive to shoot a smaller group. In my case I also learned to shoot faster and shoot as I was moving. There was always a new level of skill for one to obtain.

The minimal standard attitude could clearly be seen the last time I went into the military. I was required to do a fitness test which consists of doing as many pushups, sit-ups, as one can do in two minutes. There was also required a two mile timed run. They evaluate you to a minimum standard of fitness based on your age. Now remember the push-ups and sit-ups were timed two minutes to see however many you can do in that time period. I was asked by one of the soldiers, how many I was going to do. I said its two minutes in duration, I have no idea. He said you don't understand, the minimum standard is 28 for someone your age. On doing push-ups and sit-ups, you passed at that level. Why would I do any more than the minimum standard required he asked? I said I'm not a minimalist I want to see how many I could do. He said, but that's going to make the rest of us look bad. That is the mindset of somebody who is striving to do the minimum amount of work required to pass or to achieve. This minimalist thing has never been part of my mindset or lexicon.

 I am working to consistently improve my shooting skill. Some of the hardest skills for me to achieve with a gun is accuracy versus speed. You try to balance the speed with the accuracy to come out with the best combination you can get. There is never perfect, only something bigger, better, faster, and stronger. The goal is to achieve what rare individuals within the same field have done. It is kind of a mentor program to look at them for the level to reach. Let us first try for the standard they reached and then strive for a realistic goal for you.

Size matters in most things

 Size does matter when you are looking at the physical aspects of a person that is doing a specific type of executive protection. It is important when you are giving away your location to the public. The person the team is protecting may be a celebrity and might want attention from the public. In this case the event location is announced ahead of time. This can be a very important and necessary aspect as it is where the celebrities' income is coming from. The security team is going to need people able to handle a crowd that wants to touch or press in on your principle. Protection personnel have to keep them at a proper distance. This requires a physically larger intimidating type of person. This physical type security can hold back the people that are waiting to touch whoever is being protected. People will immediately notice those rare individuals who are bigger than average. Also protection may be picked for the sheer image that wants to be created; to be bigger, mean, intimidating, or even better looking than the average person can be an asset. As a side note, I meet President Jimmy Carter after a natural disaster in Nebraska and noticed he was shorter in stature than expected. All his security detail was the same height giving the illusion he was taller.

 Abnormally large people draw attention to themselves purely by their physical size. Their unusual looks maybe required for special details to provide physical intimidation. It is the size of the individuals not their skill level or effectiveness that takes priority. I also want to make the statement that just being big didn't stop the bad guys from knocking down the Twin Towers in New York. If again you're holding back a crowd the larger individual intimidates by size alone, providing a distinct advantage. They also are more likely to have an easier time doing the job as fewer people will want to test their abilities.

This image effect is not an advantage if you are trying to be discreet in moving a principle around without drawing public attention. A very large individual or a very good-looking individual is going to draw people's attention every time. Unwanted attention will then allow them to notice your protected person. Being very large can be an advantage as far as physically covering the principle with your body if shooting starts but it is a disadvantage for those clients who do not want public attention. On the other hand, being big also makes for an easy target. Some BUGS (big ugly guy) are very easy target for a shooter because the size alone is easy for the eye to follow as a detail moves in a crowd. They also provide a lot of square footage to shoot at for the first shot. The other way to look at things is if you don't want to be noticed, as in a ghost protocol, find someone who can blend with the crowd. In my opinion it is better not to present the target in the first place. Not being able to identify a target prevents the first shot.

People focus attention to anything out of place or things they are familiar with from media such as television. An example of a different type of Executive Protection is to be the escort of an affluent couple wanting some additional assurance of safety out on the town. They want to go out for a low pressure Saturday night. The husband is part of the reason for the security need. He played a major part in a banking company layoff. The couple feels that getting recognized in downtown big city is possible and can result in a negative situation. They want to go to a local restaurant for dinner and drinks without a problem resulting. He is going to need and hire protection for the evening. I was hired for an assignment like this. You would not want to draw attention to this couple by having a big ugly guy in attendance. The content of the contingency surrounding the principle needs to put out a good city business image so they blend into the crowd. Dressing like an Iowa farmer would not fit the corporate banking look found in the middle of most cities. A homeless image maybe good for surveillance but in this example, it would probably not be what the couple is looking for on this particular detail.

I was never further away from the couple than 50 feet for the whole night. The couple went through the downtown area to an upper level restaurant and then to a local bar. I did some clandestine filming so I could prove to the wife who was looking around trying to spot me and assure her that I had them covered the whole evening. He had looked around several times as well and did not know where I was located. It took a lot of planning and preparation that most protection units would not want to do. I put in far beyond the minimum effort required due to my mindset and my reputation in general. This type of effort to afford the best level of protection work possible had helped eliminate any trouble during that evening. I was close enough where I could have easily stepped in between the threat and the people I was protecting or escorted them out of the area. The basic principle is to provide the person being protected with a balance between doing what you're trying to achieve protection wise and what your protection looks like.

How will you react to stress?

There is a mental evaluation most individuals go though when faced with possible death. From my life, when you are being drafted for Vietnam, you have to realize and analyze all those stories you heard growing up and understand that those types of events could happen to you. The thought of being captured or tortured causes you to evaluate your life. You introspectively look at how you going to deal with this situation before you actually have to confront the possibility. This process motivates you into trying to make peace with your religion and deal with the stress.

The stress created by having a gun fired at you decreases the accuracy of your return fire. This is not a good thing when trying to stop a threat. This compromise in accuracy can be demonstrated when I was in Philadelphia a few years back. A shooting occurred between one subject and two FBI agents near the hospital I was working at. A total of forty shots were fired and nothing was hit other than the road, a few trees, and some buildings. Training in dealing with gun fire stress and overall performance under fire could have kept this event from occurring. This refers to training that wasn't invented when this example of a shootout occurred. It happened in the era before cell phones and YouTube videos. Stress shooting training has improved and the likelihood of a shootout like this has dramatically gone down. It is very important that security personnel stay up to date with new and current technologies if you are expecting to be at the top of your game. Technology doubles every two years so you have to stay within the change or lose your edge over the bad guys.

Change and adaptation to the modern violent environment is a requirement. Let me give you an analogy relating with deer hunting. The hunter is the predator and the deer is the prey. A hunter sits in a tree using new up to date technology, strategy, and planned opportunity to attempt to make a kill. The bad guy does the same only he is hunting people instead of deer. If a deer wanted to live, it must try as best as it can to avoid people sitting in trees. Hunters also use bait to make the hunting easier. When a deer sees a big pile of corn in the middle of the woods, it must instinctively avoid this bait without over thinking how it got there. The military, police, and security all train in the ability to spot predators before they can do harm. There is a need for additional experience dealing with our new fear causing modern threats and help us not only avoid the predators sitting in trees but also gives us the intuition to ignore strange new piles of bait.

Sex, not what you are thinking

Having a female as a member of you team is a very important and a very good thing. When the protected person is a female, the team member can escort the principle into places males cannot venture easily. This way the team has qualified assets on the protected principle at all times. This female member must train to the same standards as all male members do with no exceptions.

At this time, I want to cover a point that few will talk about. It is human nature to have desire for those things that protect us. We can be attracted to the person assigned to protect us due to the fact that they may be good looking, healthy, muscular, have an air of control, or just the Alpha person in charge. This type of person can be desirable, but this may lead to being a disruptive thing. If you are picking an educated respected quiet professional for a security detail based on your physical desires for them, you are doing everyone a disservice. You are putting them and yourself in danger. To do the job effectively, only professional behavior must remain and all parties focused on protection not dreaming about some type of off-duty or on-duty relationship. The relationship no matter what form it takes brings emotional baggage to the job. This is not good for maintaining a high standard of protection.

Conclusion

Precision Dynamics Group, in which I am a member, function as a highly trained Executive Protection team. We are all licensed private investigators and expertly armed and trained. Due to changing conditions in the world, we are willingly changing our skills as we upgrade our training; buy new technology, and meeting licensing standards. I am proud of this team and recommend you give us a chance to prove we are more than qualified to do the job right. The information I provided comes out of my own personal experience. I take this job very seriously. If my life was on the line, and it is with this job, I cannot afford to think about it as me being good enough. I want to go home at the end of the day knowing I gave my best. If I do not make it home at the end of the day, I want to be sure, beyond all doubt, that the person I was responsible for protecting did.

ABOUT THE AUTHOR

Dr. Willer brings a unique and successful point of view to the discussion table. Active as a Black Belt founder of American Martial Arts, served over a dozen honorable years of military police service to America, and completed a new military based novel, boredom is not part of his lexicon. With more than 20 years of diverse medical experience, Dr. Willer worked for ECPI University as a medical instructor. He holds a doctorate in Healthcare Administration from Warren National University, masters from Wayne State College in education, and is a certified cardiovascular technologist. He is currently working for Precision Dynamics Group as a Private Investigator Associate.